Animals and birds

1864

I0440144

ISBN-13 : 978-1507519738
ISBN-10 : 1507519737

Notice

This documentary study use historic, archived documents.

Because of this, some pages may look blurry or low quality.

Still are included in this book because they have

high value from critical, documentary, historical,

informative and journalistic point of view .

Dtp
and
graphic design

Iacob Adrian

Author statement

This is a series of fairy tales and stories

for children.

ANIMALS & BIRDS.

DAME WONDER'S Series

1865

Notes

ANIMALS AND BIRDS.

Notes

How sweet and gentle an animal a sheep is! and this little lamb is a great pet with this young Miss.

Notes

Robert had a pretty poney, it had a flow-
ing mane and a long tail, it was very tame
and would eat out of his hand.

Notes

Here is little Julia feeding the fowls at the garden gate; the old hen breaks the food quite small and then calls the young chickens to eat it.

Notes

The pretty spotted cow is waiting at the gate for Jane to milk her, and Charles has got his little mug ready to have a drink of nice new milk.

Notes

The plumage of the peacock is very hand-
some, he is fond of strutting about in the sun-
shine and spreading his tail out like a fan.

Notes

The Newfoundland dog is very fond of swimming in the water, and has often saved little children from being drowned

Notes

How gracefully the swans swim in the water, they are milk white, but the young ones are grey, and are called cygnets.

Notes

Bibliographic sources :

Animals and birds ([between 1864 and 1870])
Publisher: New York : McLoughlin Bro's, publishers, No. 30 Beekman Street

This documentary study use,
combined in various proportions,
elements from the following categories,
forms and subsets :
- fair use
- documentary
- documentary photography
- feature
- journalism
- arts journalism
- visual journalism
- photojournalism
- celebrity photography
in order to :
- employ material as the object of cultural critique ,
- quote to illustrate an argument or point ,
- use material in historical sequence,
providing independent opinion,
using photos, press articles, advertisements,
opinions of fans etc. ...

Notes

www.ingramcontent.com/pod-product-compliance
Lightning Source LLC
Chambersburg PA
CBHW050930290526
45792CB00002B/958